Face the Facts

War and Conflict

Aryeh S. Nusbacher

For information, address the publisher:
Raintree, 100 N. LaSalle, Suite 1200, Chicago, IL 60602

Design by Mayer Media/Mark Whitchurch
Printed and bound in China.
07 06 05 04 03
10 9 8 7 6 5 4 3 2 1

Library of Congress Cataloging-in-Publication Data

Nusbacher, Aryeh J. S., 1966-
  War and conflict / Aryeh Nusbacher.
      p. cm. -- (Face the facts)
Summary: Gives an overview of the history of war, the consequences of
war and conflict, and the rights and wrongs of both, and includes
information about terrorism, refugees, and prevention of military
violence.
Includes bibliographical references and index.
  ISBN 0-7398-6435-1 (HC), 1-4109-0048-7 (Pbk.)
  1. War--Juvenile literature. 2. Military history--Juvenile
literature. [1. War. 2. Military history.] I. Title. II. Series.
  U21.2 .N77 2003
  355.02--dc21
                                   2002013052

Acknowledgments
The publishers would like to thank the following for permission to reproduce photographs:
pp. 1, 13, 20–21 Bettmann/Corbis; pp. 4, 8 (top), 14 (bottom) 19, 37 Peter Newmark's Pictures; p. 6 Peter Connolly/AKG London; p. 7 Ancient Art and Architecture Collection; p. 8–9 Charles and Josette Lenars/Corbis; p. 10 AKG London; p. 12 Fred Ramage/Hulton Archive; pp. 14–15, 16 Photri/Topham Picturepoint; pp. 17, 22, 36, 38, 45 AP/Topham Picturepoint; p. 23 UNHCR; p. 24 Popperfoto; pp. 25, 27 Image Works/Topham Picturepoint; p. 26 (bottom) Philippe Dutoit/Sipa/Rex Features; p. 28 (top), 42 Laurent Rebours/Associated Press; pp. 28–29 Jeremy Young/Rex Features; p. 31 Sipa/Rex Features; p. 32 Martin McCullough/Rex Features; pp. 35, 47 Ian McIlgorm/Rex Features; p. 41 Ron Giling/Still Pictures; p. 49 Bill Janscha/Associated Press; pp. 50–51 Topham Picturepoint.

Cover photograph: Popperfoto

Every effort has been made to contact copyright holders of any material reproduced in this book. Any omissions will be rectified in subsequent printings if notice is given to the publishers.

Some words are shown in bold, **like this.** You can find out what they mean by looking in the Glossary.

Contents

Introduction

In any society conflict arises when different people want different things. Somehow these differences must be resolved. Sometimes conflicts can be resolved by peaceful means such as bargaining, but sometimes the situation escalates. When two sides cannot resolve their differences by peaceful means, they fight each other. When two states cannot resolve their differences peacefully, they go to **war.**

British painter Abraham Cooper (1787–1868) imagined this combat between King Richard I of England and the Kurdish general Saladin during the Third Crusade (1187–1192).

4

Sometimes conflicts are about resources such as oil, land, or minerals. In 1960–1963 the Congolese province of Katanga fought a war with Congo's government over who would control Katanga's rich mineral resources, including extensive deposits of copper and cobalt. Sometimes conflicts are about ideas. In 1096 Europe was swept up in the fervor of crusades, or Christian holy wars. Christian kings, knights, and even children went to war with people whose religious ideas differed from theirs. But these wars were often also about land, Christian holy places in and near Jerusalem, that the crusaders wanted to take from the Muslims. The crusades began with attacks on French and German Jews who, like the Muslims, had religious beliefs and customs that differed from those of the Christians. The crusaders even killed Christians in the Middle East who were religiously and culturally different from Christians in Western Europe.

Ethnic differences

Some conflicts have nothing to do with what people think or want. Sometimes people fight about who they are. A group of people who share a common culture and language, or who believe they share a common ancestry, is known as an **ethnic group.** Ethnic identity is often a positive thing, giving rise to special art, literature, clothing, and spirituality or religion. Sometimes, however, ethnic groups clash with one another simply because they are different.

Guerrilla warfare

Many people imagine war as a series of large **battles** fought on battlefields. But some groups do not have the resources to make war in this way, although they still seek to resolve conflict with violence. When these groups fight against a stronger, **regular** army or attack important economic targets, such as power stations or railroad lines, they are called **guerrilla** fighters. (Guerrilla is a Spanish word meaning "little war.")

> **❝War is merely the continuation of politics by other means.❞**
>
> The German philosopher Carl von Clausewitz (1780–1831) maintained that war was just a way to achieve political aims by using violence in an organized way.

Some groups go beyond guerrilla warfare and seek to use violence against people who cannot fight back. Someone who sets out to attack **civilians** (ordinary people) to achieve an aim is called a **terrorist.**

The Development of War

There have probably been **wars** as long as civilization has existed. The Bible tells of wars that happened more than 3,000 years ago. In ancient Greece, between 479 B.C.E. and 323 B.C.E., powerful cities were only able to go to war with each other in a very limited way. These cities were dominated by wealthy farmers, and went to war to achieve the goals of these powerful men. To protect their interests, the farmers had to carefully plan their methods of fighting. For instance, they could not give weapons to their slaves, or the slaves might use these weapons to overthrow the farmers. The cities therefore had to restrict themselves to small armies of farmers. The farmers did not want to share power with craftsmen and laborers. To avoid this they required all soldiers to wear a very expensive type of bronze breastplate called a "hoplon." Since the wealthy farmers were the only people who could afford to buy armor, they were the only people who could carry weapons and hold power.

Battles and battlefields

The soldiers were called **hoplites,** from the Greek word meaning "hoplon-wearer." Because hoplites were farmers, and farmers work hard, they could not spend a great deal of time practicing their military skills. So when hoplites went

This Greek soldier from the 400s B.C.E. is putting on his hoplon, with the shoulder pieces standing up behind him.

to war, they could do little more than stand beside each other in line to fight. Because their armor was so heavy, they could not fight for long, so they fought short **battles.**

The hoplites could only fight in lines, so they needed to fight in broad, flat places. The first thing they did when they arrived to fight their enemies was to seek out a field for battle. With a few exceptions, hoplites always fought on such battlefields. This method of combat persisted well into the 20th century.

The two opposing hoplite armies would try to drive each other off the field of battle. Eventually one of the armies would become exhausted or frightened, and would try to run from the field. The

soldiers would drop their heavy armor and weapons and run back to their town or ships. The other army would build a large pile, called a trophy, of all the discarded weapons and armor as a signal to the Greek gods that one side had won and the other had lost. This custom led to the classic concept that wars are won with a decisive victory or series of victories in battle.

❝ . . . [T]he Greeks . . . have senseless wars in which the two sides decide it is time they had a battle, march out to the smoothest and most convenient ground, and proceed to butcher one another.❞

Herodotus, Greek historian of the 400s B.C.E.

This is a carefully made copy of a Greek warship of the 400s and 300s B.C.E.

Land and Ideas

Historically land has often been seen as a far more important measure of wealth than money. A **war** about land seems like a simple idea because a piece of land is something everyone can see or understand. But sometimes wars about land also involve complex ideas. For example, beginning in 1096, Christian rulers from Europe participated in crusades. These wars were mainly meant to win control over Christian holy places. This makes the crusades seem like wars of religious ideas, but many rulers actually participated in order to gain land for their families.

In contrast, beginning in 1340, English and French kings fought wars over control of France. When the old French royal house died out in 1328, the kings of England claimed to be the rightful kings of France as well. The wars they fought, known together as the Hundred Years' War, were purely about which king would control France.

This manuscript from the 1200s depicts knights setting out on the First Crusade, 200 years before.

The Albigensian Crusade

In 1209 Pope Innocent III declared a crusade against the **Cathar** religion, which was strongest in Languedoc in the south of France. The Christian church treated the Cathar religion as an incorrect or **heretical** set of beliefs called "Albigensianism" after the town of Albi where the Cathars were well established. The Pope declared that people who joined the Christian army to fight the Cathars would earn God's forgiveness for their past sins.

The beautiful Languedoc city of Carcassone was a Cathar stronghold during the Albigensian Crusade.

After years of warfare, a new pope convinced a new king of France to join the Albigensian Crusade. In May 1226 King Louis VIII of France accepted a large cash gift from the Church and led an army southward. For the king of France, who did not rule Languedoc, this was an opportunity to seize control of a large area of rich farmland while also creating a feeling of unity among northern French Christians. By the time the Crusade ended in 1229, Louis had gone from ruling only parts of northern France to ruling territories from the English Channel to the Mediterranean.

The Albigensian Crusade shows how the same war can be fought over both territory and ideas. While the popes had started the Albigensian Crusade as a war of ideas, Louis had fought for land, to bring more of France under his control, and for money.

Industry and War

The first rifles, produced in the 1500s, were handmade by master craftsmen and their apprentices. Only rich men could afford to buy these weapons, and they were certainly not prepared to send them off to **war** with soldiers who might break or lose them. Instead, soldiers were armed with cheaper but less accurate muskets. However, by the end of the Civil War in 1865, hundreds of thousands of soldiers were armed with rifles that were being produced in large quantities.

Revolution

The event that brought about this change between the 16th and 19th centuries was the **Industrial Revolution.** In the 1800s one worker at a machine could produce many rifles where before it had taken many craftsmen to make one weapon. The industrialization of Europe also changed the mobilization of war. In 1812 soldiers of the French emperor, Napoleon Bonaparte, marched to war along the tree-shaded avenues of rural France. In 1870 Bonaparte's nephew Napoleon III sent his army to war by train. For the first time in history, huge numbers of troops could be moved very quickly, and **telegraph** wires along the railroad tracks enabled generals to stay in touch with their political leaders.

In 1814 there was no reason to have an army of a million soldiers since no army could afford a million weapons. But by 1914 a million rifles, tents, water bottles, and pairs of shoes could be quickly made in factories. A million men could be fed, clothed, armed, and transported to battlefields.

Soldiers fight with rifles in the Civil War.

World War I

When Austria-Hungary attacked Serbia in 1914, Russia mobilized its vast army to help its **ally,** Serbia. When the messages began to go out over Russian telegraph wires to summon **reservists** to railroad stations, Germany (Austria-Hungary's ally) reacted. Expecting a short war, the Germans declared war on Russia and Russia's ally, France. The German Kaiser (emperor) expected his war with France to take two or three weeks.

The Kaiser was wrong. Between 1914 and 1918, 20 million people died in the industrialized World War I. Germany had tremendous industrial potential, but so did the British and French empires. In 1917 the United States entered the war on the side of Great Britain and France, lending them its vast industrial output.

After four years of war, German **civilians** were starving and the army was running out of food and equipment. German farmers could not compete with the farmers of the British Empire, France, and the United States. German factories could not produce at the same level as British, French, and U.S. industry. The war could not be sustained, and Germany asked for a **cease-fire.**

World War II

World War II (1939–1945) was fought between two alliances. Japan, Germany, and Italy—the **Axis**—sought to build empires ruled over by **dictators.** Britain, France, Russia, the United States (after 1941), and their **allies** sought to stop them. As with World War I, it was an industrialized war; but it was far more a war of ideas than the first world war had been.

The Cold War

Even before the end of World War II, the uneasy relationship between the Western allies (notably France, the United States, and the countries of the British **Commonwealth**)

and the **Soviet Union** was worsening. Soon after the war, the Western allies confronted their wartime ally, the Soviet Union, ruled by the dictator Joseph Stalin.

Stalin was afraid that the Western allies would join together to attack the Soviet Union. The West, on the other hand, feared the spread of **communism.** Each side thought the other wanted to rule the world.

During World War II, the United States had developed the first **atomic** weapons, with the Soviet Union following close behind. Atomic weapons were far more destructive than the **conventional** and

German civilians clamber out of air-raid shelters during the Allied invasion of Germany in World War II.

chemical **weapons** used during previous wars. As each side made newer, more powerful atomic weapons, the other side kept pace. The aircraft and missiles became so fast that each side was prepared to attack the other at a signal, without waiting for confirmation that the other side was attacking. Like the great European powers in 1914, the two sides were closely matched and capable of enormous destruction.

By the 1970s each side had amassed enough weapons to destroy the world several times over. According to the scientist Carl Sagan, the aftermath of a nuclear war could include great clouds of dust blocking the sun's light from the entire Earth, with a dark "nuclear winter" destroying all life on the planet.

The distrust between East and West became known as the "Cold War." Both the Soviet Union and the Western allies knew, however, that if they went to war, the ensuing devastation would destroy both sides. This idea was called "Mutually Assured Destruction" or "MAD." It ensured that, although the two sides prepared for nearly 35 years to fight World War III, they never actually did so.

Although the United States and the Soviet Union could not safely fight each other during the Cold War, they sometimes allowed their allies to go to war. In 1973, for example, Egypt and Syria (supported by the Soviet Union) went to war with Israel (supported by the United States). The Cold War continued in this way until the collapse of the Soviet Union in 1991.

❝I know not with what weapons World War III will be fought, but World War IV will be fought with sticks and stones.❞

Scientist and inventor Albert Einstein (1879–1955), predicting the impact of a possible nuclear war on humanity

This test of a nuclear weapon shows the "mushroom cloud" that rises over the blast.

The Vietnam War

In the early 1960s the anticommunist government of South Vietnam was in danger of falling to a communist **guerrilla** movement. Many Vietnamese from North and South agreed with the communists' goal of unifying Vietnam and were not interested in the politics of **communism** and **capitalism.**

The U.S. government sent advisors to help teach the South Vietnamese soldiers to do their jobs. As the **war** started to go against South Vietnam, the United States, with help from South Korea and Australia, sent more soldiers and equipment until, by 1965, they were full participants in the war.

Although U.S. decision makers tried hard to limit the Vietnam War, for soldiers like this U.S. machine gunner and his Vietnamese communist enemies the war was long and deadly.

These Vietnamese communist fighters, taken prisoner by U.S. Marines, are being marched into captivity.

The United States was concerned that if the war became too fierce, it could involve other nations, even the **Soviet Union.** The United States was determined not to allow the war in Vietnam to turn the Cold War into World War III.

The U.S. government made every effort to keep the war from affecting daily life at home. When they discovered that the North Vietnamese received their supplies by a road that ran through neighboring Laos and Cambodia, the U.S. forces took care to attack the road in secret because they did not want to draw more countries into the conflict. The United States did not bring all their military might to bear on Vietnam stating clearly that they only wished to help preserve South Vietnam and did not wish to take over North Vietnam.

However, by 1968 Americans began to feel that they were no longer winning this war. Some U.S. decision makers feared that if they continued to fight in Vietnam, the public would demand that they send more soldiers and use more powerful weapons. This, they believed, could lead to World War III with the Soviet Union, a disaster they were desperate to avoid.

Instead, U.S. troops tried to get the South Vietnamese to defend themselves so the Americans could leave. By 1973 the last American soldiers had left Vietnam. But even with a new ruler, the South Vietnamese could not resist the popularity and military strength of the communists, and in 1975 Vietnam was unified under a communist government. The special conditions of the Cold War had helped to create a complex and costly war in Vietnam, fought amid rising unpopularity at home and causing many Americans to distrust and protest against their government.

Regulars and Irregulars

Soldiers who fight for their country, receive pay, and follow military rules are called **regulars.** This term comes from the Latin word *regula*, which means "rule." Some regular soldiers are conscripts, drafted or "conscripted" into the army for a set period of time. Other regular soldiers are professionals who expect soldiering to be their career and intend to continue in the military profession for many years.

Shaka Zulu

Regular armies are not simply a feature of Western warfare. The powerful leader Shaka Zulu (1785–1828) created a regular army that he used to lay claim to the Zulu state in southern Africa. Shaka's soldiers were expected to follow rules. They were all required to live together in the same house, although each regiment had its own living space. All the soldiers' weapons were identical. Soldiers who broke the rules were punished with death.

Shaka's "Zulu" army had an advantage over warriors from other African clans and nations because it was a regular army in a region in which most armies were not made up of regular soldiers. Because Shaka had a regular army, he was able to create the vast state of Zululand, which lasted for just over 50 years.

These officer cadets of the United States Military Academy at West Point are celebrating the end of their training to be regular army officers.

Soldiers who are not regulars are sometimes called **irregulars.** During the period of British rule in India (1755–1947), for example, the British found that, although some tribes of Indian horsemen made excellent soldiers, they were not happy under the strict discipline of the regular army. These men were recruited as irregular **cavalry,** and had their own rules. Irregulars were often more effective at certain jobs than regular cavalry soldiers.

❝The conventional army loses if it does not win. The guerrilla wins if he does not lose.❞

Henry Kissinger, then U.S. National Security Advisor, January 1969

"RPG kids"

Regular soldiers do not always have the advantage over irregulars. When Israel invaded Lebanon in 1982, they marched with a regular army. They had the very best of modern equipment and training, and expected their heavily armored tanks and armored personnel carriers (APCs) to protect them from attack.

However, as the Israelis passed through Lebanese villages, they found themselves attacked by young Palestinian fighters armed with simple antitank weapons in the form of rocket-propelled grenades (RPGs). These "RPG kids" would drive their ordinary **civilian** vehicles out of alleys, fire at Israeli vehicles, and then disappear into the maze of back streets before the Israelis could react.

These irregular fighters walk through Beirut, Lebanon, in 1982. The pipelike weapons they carry are RPG launchers.

17

Wars Between Armies

Some modern **wars,** like ancient wars, have been wars between armies. When the United States went to war with Spain in 1898, the U.S. army and navy fought what is called a **conventional** war: the armies of the two nations faced each other in **battles,** and the navies faced each other at sea. When the United States went to war again almost twenty years later in 1917, their army joined the armies of the **Allies** in World War I to fight conventional war against the German and Austria-Hungarian armies.

The Falkland Islands War

The British call a small group of islands in the South Atlantic the Falklands. Argentina knows them as the Malvinas. Since the early 19th century, Argentina and Britain had both laid claim to the islands. For years negotiations were held concerning the future of the islands, but neither side would give up its claim.

In 1982, with Argentina's corrupt dictatorship facing opposition at home, the country's military leaders decided to go to war. They thought that war would unite the people of Argentina against a common enemy. Instead of hating and resenting the cruel and ruthless government and its secret police, the Argentine people would instead focus their hatred and resentment on the British.

Invasion and response

When the Argentines invaded the islands on April 2, 1982, the British response was quick. Ships packed with soldiers set sail for the South Atlantic. The British government declared that any unfriendly ships near the islands would be sunk by Britain's Royal Navy. While the British ships sailed slowly across thousands of miles of sea, the Argentines prepared to defend the islands.

18

These British regular soldiers are marching across East Falkland Island toward Stanley, the capital of the Falklands. All the British and some of the Argentine soldiers in the war were professionals.

A conventional war

When the British ships arrived, the war began in earnest. Argentine aircraft sank British warships and **merchant ships;** British aircraft sank Argentine warships and merchant ships. The **regular** soldiers of one army fought with and killed the regulars of the other army. After 72 days the commander of the Argentine forces surrendered, and both he and his army were permitted to return home. Argentina had failed to win the islands from British rule.

A Greek commander of the Classical period would have understood the war completely. The ships had changed, the weapons had changed; but the war was still conventional: two opposing armies meeting on a field of battle.

Weapons of Mass Destruction

All weapons are designed to damage their victims—that is what weapons are meant to do. Some weapons of **war** are capable of killing masses of people at once, with no distinction between soldiers and **civilians** or between important targets and unimportant ones. These are called "weapons of mass destruction."

Poison gas, biological warfare, and atomic bombs

Chemical weapons are poisons, usually poison gas or mist. During World War I, both sides developed poison gas weapons and began using them in 1915. Another technique of mass destruction introduced during World War I was **biological warfare.** Such weapons attack the enemy by infecting them with a disease such as anthrax.

During World War II, scientists from around the world developed the **atomic bomb.** The first atomic bombs were tested and used in the summer of 1945. The first **hydrogen bombs** were tested in 1952, but they have never been used in war.

Weapons of mass destruction have been used recently, for example, during the Iran-Iraq War (1980–1988). In this war both the Iranians and the Iraqis began to use poison gas against each other. In 1987 the Iraqi government used poison gas as part of a campaign against the Kurdish people in northern Iraq, killing civilian adults and children.

Extremist groups

Although there is concern that countries may use weapons of mass destruction against their enemies, threats from non-state groups could be more dangerous. While even **dictators** may be deterred from using weapons of mass destruction if they know that their enemies might use similar weapons in return, some extremist groups are harder to threaten.

Aum Shinrikyo is a religious **cult** based in Japan. The group believes that the world will end soon, and that it is a good idea to help the world end sooner. There is evidence to suggest that members of Aum Shinrikyo released microbes that cause anthrax and botulism (two deadly diseases) in Japan in 1993. In 1995 the group attempted to commit mass murder by introducing a poison gas into Tokyo's underground railway system. Twelve people were killed by the gas and about 5000 were injured.

The United States has many enemies. It is also very powerful. People thinking they have no other way to attack the United States might smuggle nuclear weapons into the country to cause death, radiation poisoning, and fear. The threat of such action by extremist groups has led the United States to invest in equipment that can detect small amounts of nuclear material.

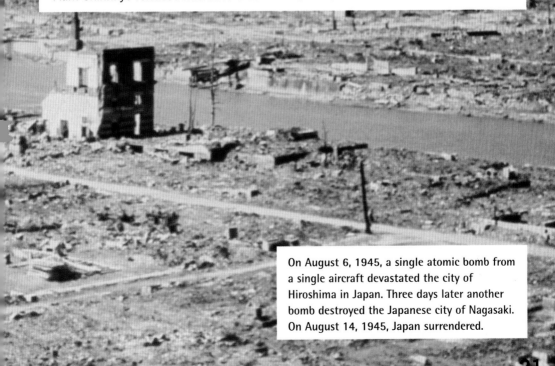

On August 6, 1945, a single atomic bomb from a single aircraft devastated the city of Hiroshima in Japan. Three days later another bomb destroyed the Japanese city of Nagasaki. On August 14, 1945, Japan surrendered.

21

Ethnic and Religious Conflicts

An **ethnic group** is made up of people who share a history and culture. Often an ethnic group will also share a language, a national costume, or a religion. Sometimes an ethnic group will have a particularly close tie to a piece of land. One example is the Basque ethnic group in Spain. Some Basques insist that they must have a state of their own. A very small group of Basques conduct a campaign of violent **terrorism** against the Spanish government in support of ethnic self-rule.

Kosovo

Throughout history people have migrated, and the same piece of land can often be important to more than one ethnic group. The province of Kosovo is in the state of Serbia in the former Yugoslavia and is settled mostly by ethnic Albanians who speak the Albanian language, write with the Roman alphabet, and are mostly Muslim. The province also has a population of Serbs, ethnic Slavs who speak Serbo-Croatian, write with the Cyrillic alphabet, and are mostly Orthodox Christians.

In 1389 a Serb army fought the armies of the Turkish sultan in Kosovo. The site of this battle is important to Serbs as a symbol of their fight against the Turks, and also of the Christians' fight with the Muslims for control of the region.

The policeman on the left is fighting with an ethnic Albanian rioter in the Kosovo province in 1998.

From 1974 to 1989, Kosovo had self-rule within Yugoslavia, and many Kosovar Albanians felt that they should have self-rule again. But Serbia, the largest and strongest state in Yugoslavia, was not willing to return Kosovo to self-rule. Many Serbs felt that Serbia should control Kosovo because of its importance to their people.

In 1998 the Serbs of Kosovo feared that the **United Nations (UN)** would divide the province into Serb and Albanian areas. To increase the amount of Serb-held territory, they began to drive Albanians from their homes. Serbs murdered many Kosovar Albanians and buried them in mass graves.

In 1999 the North Atlantic Treaty Organization **(NATO)** forced the Serbian leadership to move its army and secret police out of Kosovo. Since then Kosovo has remained part of Serbia, but with special status. NATO soldiers remain in Kosovo to ensure that Serbia does not attempt to return the province to Serbian control. The NATO soldiers and UN police in Kosovo try to get the Serbians and Albanians of Kosovo to live together in peace. The interethnic conflict in Kosovo is small, but at least as brutal and complex as a full-scale war.

These ethnic Albanian refugees are arriving in United Nations camps in the former Yugoslav republic of Macedonia.

War Crimes

Acts that are illegal in peacetime, such as shooting or bombing, become legal in wartime. As long as a soldier commits the act, shooting an enemy soldier in the head is not murder; and hitting an enemy soldier in the head is not assault. In fact, soldiers in wartime are often rewarded for doing things that they would be punished for doing in peacetime. Some deeds, however, are so horrible that they are considered crimes even in wartime. A **war crime** is killing or destruction that breaks the laws of **war,** and that is not required to achieve military aims.

Genocide

The laws of war govern the way soldiers behave when fighting. They also govern the treatment of **civilians**, prisoners, medics, and property. During World War II, Germany broke the laws of war by committing **genocide** (mass murder) against Jews and other **ethnic groups.** After the war German leaders were put on trial in Nuremberg, where a **tribunal** (court) ruled on whether each one was guilty of war crimes. Some of those found guilty were hanged and some were imprisoned.

Some war criminals escaped from Germany before they could be put on trial. Adolph Eichmann, one of the men who planned the genocide of Europe's Jews, fled to Argentina. The State of Israel (created shortly after World War II as a homeland for the Jews) tracked him down and smuggled him to Jerusalem, where he stood trial for war crimes. The Israeli court convicted Eichmann and he was hanged in 1962.

Nazi mass murderer Adolph Eichmann stands to hear an Israeli court announce that he has been found guilty of war crimes.

❝I think that technologies are morally neutral until we apply them. It's only when we use them for good or for evil that they become good or evil.❞

Author William Gibson, November 23, 1994

The skulls of ethnic Tutsis murdered by ethnic Hutus in the Rwanda genocide of 1994 are kept in place as a memorial.

Massacres

In 1982 when Ariel Sharon was Israel's defense minister, Israel invaded Lebanon. One of the main reasons for the invasion was to help put a Lebanese **militia** called the Christian Falange in control of Lebanon. This move, Sharon hoped, would end Palestinian attacks on Israel from Lebanon.

The Israelis took control of several Palestinian **refugee** camps in Lebanon. The Christian Falange stormed into the Sabra and Shatilla refugee camps near Beirut and **massacred** between 700 and 800 people. Those killed were mainly **Palestine Liberation Organization (PLO)** and militia fighters, but the number also included 15 women and 20 children.

An Israeli commission of inquiry concluded that Sharon had some responsibility for the massacre because Israeli troops did not stop the killing, but it decided that he was not a war criminal. The Christian Falangist leader Elie Hobeika, who probably was responsible for the massacre, was never charged or punished. He lived in Lebanon until he was murdered in 2002.

Recently, war crimes tribunals have met to try people accused of crimes against humanity in Rwanda and the former Yugoslavia. The tribunals have found it difficult to force people to stand trial. The **United Nations** managed to bring former Yugoslav president Slobodan Milosevic to trial, but it is harder to find the people who ordered and carried out the killings.

The Consequences of Conflict

For the people who live in a **war** zone, war does not simply go away when a **cease-fire** is declared. It is almost 100 years since World War I littered the fields of Belgium with craters, yet every year Belgian farmers' plows turn up bodies, equipment, and, worst of all, unexploded **shells.** Often the shells are still dangerous, and army experts are called in to destroy them.

Land mines

Land mines are explosive devices that are buried underground. When a person or a vehicle triggers the mine, it explodes. Small mines (called antipersonnel mines) can kill a person. Larger mines can destroy vehicles, even tanks.

❝Land mines are uniquely savage in the history of modern conventional warfare not only because of their appalling individual impact, but also their long-term social and economic destruction.❞

Graça Machel, UN Secretary General's Expert on the Impact of Armed Conflict on Children, in the Machel Report, 1994

When **regular armies** finish fighting, their engineers are expected to find and remove their land mines. **Irregular armies** are not so careful. Today thousands of land mines remain in former war zones. Animals sometimes trigger mines by walking across them. Children sometimes trigger them while playing. It is estimated that 30 to 40 percent of land mine victims in the world are younger than fifteen years of age.

In 1996 there were an estimated 10 million land mines in Cambodia. These young Cambodians (below) are victims of mine explosions.

Cluster bombs

Other dangerous devices litter former battlefields. Cluster bombs are made up of many small "bomblets." Each of these is filled with an explosive, and when they explode the damage is greater than that of a single bomb. Sometimes bomblets are defective and they fail to explode when they are supposed to. Cluster bombs resemble a small football, and when children find them they often play with them. The bomb may then explode, killing or wounding the children.

Toxic smoke billows from the oil wells of Kuwait, blown up by retreating Iraqis at the end of the Gulf War in 1991.

Dangerous chemicals

Chemicals used in explosives or in fuels are often left in war zones. Some people have claimed that dust from the bullets used in some guns during the Gulf War (1990–1991) has made them ill. Some scientists suggest that the insect spray used to prevent the spread of disease in military camps poisoned soldiers who were fighting in the Gulf War.

In war, many important targets can involve chemicals. Explosives may hit factories where weapons and explosives are made or where consumer goods like plastics or aluminum are produced, causing chemicals used in manufacturing or toxic waste products to be spread over wide areas, poisoning the air and water.

Damage to the environment can hurt people directly. In many parts of the world, a single cow or sheep is an important part of a family's wealth. If it is killed by a land mine or poisoned by chemicals released in an explosion, a family can be ruined, sometimes to the point of starvation.

Casualties

Civilian casualties

War brings disaster to people who are not involved in the fighting. The casualties of war include not only the lives of young people, but also the loss of their potential contributions to their families and to society.

In World War I, British soldiers learned to rush out of the trenches in little groups called "blobs" in the hope of avoiding being hit.

This boy, being carried to safety by a Red Cross worker, was wounded in fighting between two **guerrilla** groups in Colombia.

On July 1, 1916, 753 men of the Royal Newfoundland Regiment marched across a short distance of open ground in France. They were part of the British army that was conducting the Battle of the Somme against the Germans in World War I. The Newfoundlanders met with a wall of German machine-gun fire. Within a half-hour, 710 of the men had been killed, wounded, or were missing.

Newfoundland is an island off the coast of Canada, now part of the Canadian province of Newfoundland and Labrador. At the start of World War I, Newfoundland's population was about 250,000. When Britain became involved in the war, Newfoundland was expected to contribute to the war effort, and 5,482 men and women went overseas to help. More than a third of Newfoundland's young men joined the armed forces to fight. During the four years of war, 1,500 Newfoundlanders were killed and 2,300 were wounded.

The special conditions of World War I resulted in a rapid and devastating spread of disease. Measles, mumps, and pneumonia rampaged through the units of soldiers living close together in the dirty conditions of trenches and troopships. Eventually about 7,500 Newfoundlanders would die of diseases contracted as a result of the war.

"The Lost Generation"

Newfoundland was profoundly affected by the loss of so many of its young people, especially the young male soldiers. The tightly knit island community had lost about 9,000 people in the space of five years. Until new families could be raised, there was a shortage of people to do important jobs, a shortage of parents for children, and a shortage of husbands and wives for young people growing up.

Worldwide the generation of World War I was sometimes referred to as "The Lost Generation," a term first used by the American writer Gertrude Stein. She was referring not only to the people who had been lost in the war, but also to the people who had survived, living with the loss of their friends and families.

Refugees

Whatever way they may feel about the reasons for **war,** ordinary people do not feel safe when bullets are whizzing past them and into their houses. Often people must move away from a war zone for their own safety. When people leave their homes they become **refugees.** They need a place to sleep and a source of food and water. The **United Nations** High Commissioner for Refugees and other United Nations organizations establish camps for refugees and try to provide for their basic needs.

Ethnic cleansing

During the Bosnian Civil War (1991–1995), Bosnian Muslims, Serbs, and Croats wanted to create areas with people from only one **ethnic group.** In a process called "ethnic cleansing," ethnic groups deliberately destroyed the homes of people from other ethnic groups to make them refugees. If they did not leave, they were often attacked or murdered. The refugees had to move elsewhere in Bosnia, sometimes elsewhere in Europe. This **transfer of population** is illegal under international law, but it is difficult to prevent.

During the Israeli War of Independence (1948–1949), many Arabs living in formerly British-ruled Palestine left their homes. Some people left because they heard broadcasts on Arab radio stations telling them to leave temporarily, promising they could come back when the war was over. Some left because they feared that the Israelis would harm them. Others left because they knew that, in war, innocent **civilians** are often killed or injured by accident.

When the war was over, the Israelis refused to allow the Arab refugees to return to their homes. They told them to settle in the Arab sector of Palestine, then controlled by Jordan and Egypt.

The building of permanent homes for Palestinian refugees is illegal under international law because it represents a transfer of population. Arab countries have been unwilling to give homes to the Palestinians, possibly because it is useful for them to have a large population of refugees demanding the destruction of Israel. The United Nations Relief and Works Agency for Palestine has provided refugee camps for the Palestinian refugees, and many have lived in these camps ever since leaving Palestine.

This woman from Khan Younis in the Palestinian Authority's Gaza Strip is old enough to have known British, Egyptian, and Israeli occupation.

Terrorism

Terrorism is the purposeful murder or maiming of the innocent and defenseless to inspire fear in order to achieve political goals. A **guerrilla** or a soldier might accidentally kill innocent people, but **terrorists** *plan* to kill people who are not a direct threat to them.

Terrorists are people who find that their goals cannot be achieved through peaceful means or even through guerrilla warfare. Often their aims cannot be achieved at all. Because they cannot gain support for their aims through positive means, they gain attention and support through negative means. Because people are less frightened by attacks against soldiers, who have weapons and can defend themselves, terrorists choose to attack **civilians.**

The terrorist relies on the media to spread fear. If people did not know that the violence took place, they would not be afraid. To the media, however, terrorism is news, and it is their duty to report it. Some governments do not allow the media to report failed terrorist incidents or to broadcast terrorist demands, hoping that, without the publicity they count on, the terrorists will fail in their aims. Other governments, such as the United States, are not permitted under law to engage in such censorship.

Security forces survey the damage after terrorists of the "Real IRA" exploded a bomb in Omagh, Northern Ireland, in 1998, killing 29 civilians.

❝Kill one, frighten a thousand.❞

Sun Tzu, Chinese general and philosopher of war, c. 500 B.C.E.

Some governments use terrorists to attack their enemies and to manipulate world affairs. This is called "state-sponsored terrorism." Some state sponsors of terrorism provide money or training for terrorists and allow them to set up offices and recruit others openly. They provide a safe place where terrorists can hide when other governments are pursuing them.

Some criminals use terrorism to frighten governments into allowing them to operate businesses. For example, the drug producers of Colombia use terrorism to cripple the nation's criminal justice system by murdering and intimidating people employed in it. This is called "narco-terrorism."

There is a slogan among those who support terrorists: "One man's terrorist is another man's freedom fighter." This slogan says that because terrorists often claim to fight for freedom, they should be considered better than ordinary criminals. Those who oppose terrorists first point out that terrorism can be a means of achieving any number of goals: freedom, power, or money. Second, they assert that while a very few people have used terror to achieve freedom for themselves and others, most terrorists fight for their own power and influence.

Al-Qaeda

In 1978 a **communist** government controlled Afghanistan, supported since late 1979 by the army of the **Soviet Union.** People from around the Muslim world came to help Afghans who fought to get the Soviets out. These resistance groups were supported by the United States and other countries. One of the resistance leaders was Osama bin Laden of Saudi Arabia. He was an organizer and a wealthy man who was able to channel money from other sources to support his cause.

When the Soviet Union withdrew its army from Afghanistan in 1989, many of the resistance fighters found it difficult to go home and return to normal life. Some missed the feeling of power that came from fighting; some missed the feeling of freedom that came from living in the hills. Others missed the sense of mission that came with fighting to eject non-Muslims from a Muslim land. Although some of the fighters came from deprived backgrounds, many were wealthy young men used to money and privilege.

Osama bin Laden brought many of the fighters together to continue their violent way of life outside Afghanistan. They formed a new group that would seek to end American influence in Muslim countries and to destroy the State of Israel. They also hope to impact the rulers of Arab nations such as Saudi Arabia. Because they could not succeed by means of **conventional war,** they would fight with terror by killing Americans and Jews.

The group soon became known as "al-Qaeda ul-Sullbah," Arabic for "the firm base,"or "al-Qaeda" (the base) for short. In 1998 bin Laden merged al-Qaeda with an Egyptian group called al-Jihad (meaning "the holy war") with similar goals. The new al-Qaeda was backed by many of the same people who had supported the resistance in its fight against the Soviet Union.

In 1998 al-Qaeda became known worldwide when it bombed American embassies in Africa, killing hundreds of people.

On September 11, 2001, civilian airliners were hijacked by members of al-Qaeda, who flew them into the World Trade Center (a large office complex in New York) and the Pentagon (U.S. defense headquarters in Washington, D.C.). Thousands of **civilians** were killed. The United States and its **allies** responded by destroying al-Qaeda's bases in Afghanistan and by pledging to seek out and destroy **terrorism** everywhere.

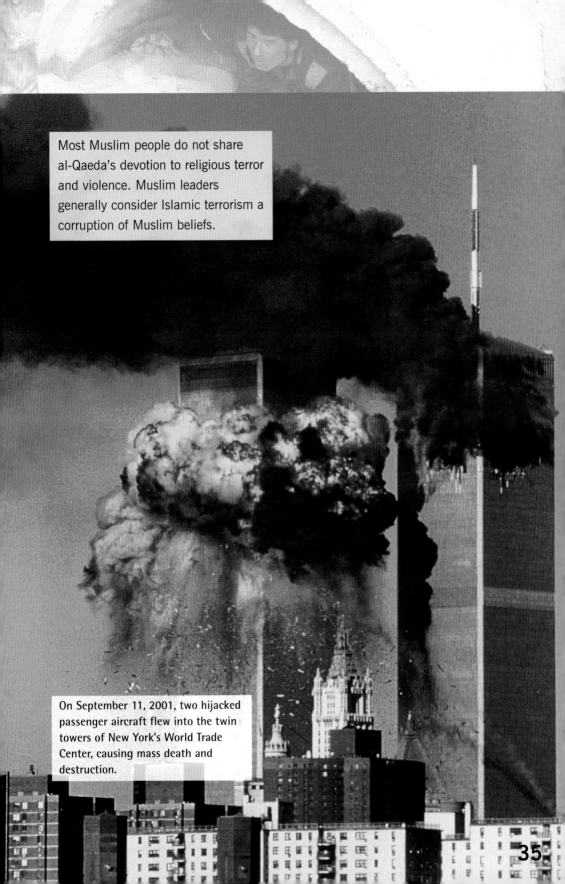

Most Muslim people do not share al-Qaeda's devotion to religious terror and violence. Muslim leaders generally consider Islamic terrorism a corruption of Muslim beliefs.

On September 11, 2001, two hijacked passenger aircraft flew into the twin towers of New York's World Trade Center, causing mass death and destruction.

War and Peace

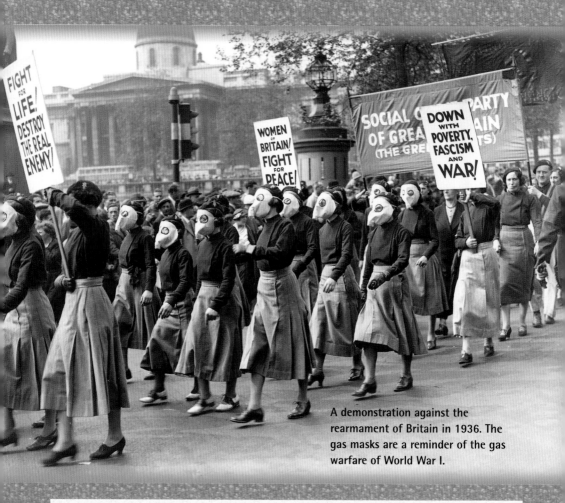

A demonstration against the rearmament of Britain in 1936. The gas masks are a reminder of the gas warfare of World War I.

Most states hate going to **war.** War brings death, destruction, and ruin. It is expensive and wasteful. Failure in war can bring national embarrassment, as the United States found in the years after the war in Vietnam. Even success in war can lead to unexpected outcomes. U.S. President George Bush was very popular at the time of the Gulf War, but only a few months later he was defeated in an election.

Many people believe that because war is horrible, it must be avoided at all costs. They believe that no matter how bad the alternative, war is always the wrong choice. This idea is known as pacifism. The horror of World War I made pacifism a popular idea in Europe. Millions of deaths in war had convinced many that anything was better than that. Then they faced the threat of Adolph Hitler and **Nazi Germany.**

Taking over Europe

Some Europeans in the 1800s imagined that they were part of an **ethnic group** called the "Aryan race." Long before Hitler became dictator of Germany in 1934, he planned to build a vast super-state for the Aryan race. According to Hitler and his followers, the Aryans were a race of rulers that would rule over all of Europe, using other "inferior peoples" as their slaves.

When Hitler's Germany became strong enough, he began to take over other countries. In 1938 the Germans took over Austria. Later in the year, they invaded Czechoslovakia (now the Czech Republic and Slovakia). Britain and France pledged to defend Czechoslovakia. Some people suggested that it was essential to stop Hitler, and that the only way to stop him was to go to war. The pacifist feeling in Europe said that anything was better than war, and even those who opposed Hitler were not united. So Hitler was able to seize part of Czechoslovakia. This victory encouraged him to take the rest of Czechoslovakia, and to invade Poland the following year, thus starting World War II.

In 1938 Germany was not strong enough to stand up to an alliance of Poland, Czechoslovakia, Britain, and France. But Britain and France left Hitler alone in part because they were afraid to start a war. Their delays allowed Nazi Germany to become powerful enough to defeat Poland and France and nearly cripple Britain. Hitler taught the nations of Europe that sometimes the only way to end a war is to fight a war.

Adolph Hitler stands on a balcony at a Nazi rally in 1933, shortly before becoming Germany's dictator.

37

Unsafe haven: Srebrenica

In the summer of 1995, a group of nations was trying to keep the peace in the former Yugoslav republic of Bosnia-Herzegovina. The nations were armed, but they were not prepared to fight. In this case, not fighting allowed the **massacres** of Srebrenica.

During the Bosnian Civil War of 1991–1995, Bosnia's Serb, Croat, and Muslim **ethnic groups** fought each other, each trying to carve out a section of Bosnia for its own people. **Refugees** fled from the region into the rest of Europe. The **United Nations** looked for places closer to home where people could safely go. In 1993 the United Nations Security Council declared the Bosnian town of Srebrenica to be a "safe haven" where Bosniacs (Bosnian Muslims) could be safe from Croats and Serbs.

The Serbs wanted Srebrenica to be part of a Bosnian Serb area, and they wanted to get rid of the Bosniacs. In the summer of 1995, the Bosnian Serb

In Srebrenica, 1996, an investigator marks each body in a mass grave with a red flag.

army began **shelling** the town of Srebrenica. The people of the town, including Bosniac soldiers and **civilians,** fled to nearby United Nations camps.

Several thousand Bosnian Muslims arrived at a Dutch **peacekeepers'** camp in the village of Potocari. Ratko Mladic, the commander of the Bosnian Serb army, told the Dutch and the Bosniacs that if the able-bodied Bosniac men surrendered, they would not be harmed. Outnumbered by the Serb army, the Dutch peacekeepers helped Mladic and his soldiers select the men and take them away. The peacekeepers then fled to their support base at Zagreb in Croatia. The Serb army took the Bosniac men away and massacred them.

Mladic and his soldiers then returned to Potocari and began killing more of the Bosniacs. They only stopped killing when the remaining Bosniacs begged to leave Srebrenica. It is estimated that six to eight thousand Bosniacs were killed in the Srebrenica area.

At Srebrenica the peacekeepers, too few and too weak in the face of the Serbs, did not fight. They kept the peace, and helped to arrange for the Bosniac men and boys to be sent to

> **"**The . . . lesson of Srebrenica is that a deliberate and systematic attempt to terrorize, expel, or murder an entire people must be met decisively with all necessary means. . . . **"**
>
> The UN Secretary General's report on the fall of Srebrenica

their deaths. The result was that the Bosnian Serbs were able to achieve their goals "peacefully"— by mass murder.

The International Criminal **Tribunal** for the former Yugoslavia charged Ratko Mladic and his boss Radovan Karadzic with **genocide,** crimes against humanity, and violating the laws of **war.** Yugoslavia and the Serb presence in Bosnia have refused to hand them over to the tribunal, so neither of them has stood trial for their crimes.

Peacekeepers are not supposed to take sides between the warring parties in a conflict, but neither should they remain neutral when deciding between right and wrong. On April 16, 2002, the entire Dutch government resigned from office in disgrace for failing to prevent the Srebrenica massacre.

39

Is War Itself the Enemy?

For hundreds of years, people have agreed that **wars** are bad, but wars are still fought. Although medieval Christian culture taught that war was glorious and manly, some medieval churchmen suggested that wars should only be fought on certain days of the week. First, they said, there should be no fighting on Sundays, the Christian day of rest and worship. Then they extended this "**truce of God**" to Thursdays, Fridays, and Saturdays. This did not bring peace; people just fought harder on Mondays, Tuesdays, and Wednesdays.

A just war?

The Christian **theologian** and lawyer Thomas Aquinas (1226–1274) said that only proper authorities, such as governments, should wage war. He also said that war was only to be waged in a **just cause** and with good intentions. In other words, leaders could only take their people to war to achieve peace and justice in the end.

Aquinas said that it is right to wage a **just war.** From Aquinas's time to World War I, war was considered simply a way for nations to settle their differences. After the tragedy of World War I, however, the nations of the world began to consider war itself to be wrong.

Efforts to ban war

In 1919 the **League of Nations** agreed that member states would try every possible alternative before going to war. In 1928 the Kellogg-Briand Pact was signed by the most powerful states in the world. The nations who signed the pact (agreement) said they would never go to war again. The pact effectively outlawed war, yet every nation that agreed to the Kellogg-Briand Pact (except Ireland) went to war between 1939 and 1945.

When the **United Nations** was formed in 1945, its charter said that states no longer had the right to go to war: only the United Nations itself had the right. This charter has not succeeded in outlawing war. Since 1945 numerous member states of the United Nations have fought wars.

The United Nations Security Council sits in session in New York.

❝Last night I had the strangest dream, I never dreamed before. I dreamed the world had all agreed to put an end to war.❞

Canadian folksinger Ed McCurdy, 1950

Right and Wrong in War

In 1604 the Dutch diplomat Hugo Grotius (1583–1645) published a book called *On the Law of War and Peace*. It suggested that a **war** did not only have to be just, it also had to be conducted in the right way. He suggested that there should be a set of rules that armies should follow when they are fighting.

Grotius said, for instance, that some things should not be destroyed in war. Fruit trees, churches, and works of art should be left untouched. Prisoners should not be sold into slavery. These were the first workable rules to govern the conduct of war.

Saudi troops search a surrendering Iraqi soldier during the Gulf War, 1991.

The Geneva **conventions (treaties),** first agreed to in 1864, and the later Hague conventions laid down a more complete set of rules for the conduct of war. The conventions protected noncombatants (people not involved in fighting), governed the treatment of prisoners and the wounded, and banned some weapons as barbaric. These conventions are not merely an attempt to make war more pleasant; they aim to keep the amount of unnecessary killing as small as possible. The conventions are enforced by courts made up of judges from different countries.

Surrender

In battle, if fighting is hopeless, soldiers must feel safe putting their hands up and surrendering. If they know that they can surrender without being robbed or murdered, they can give up rather than fight until they are killed. If surrendering is safe, then the fighting can end sooner.

To make surrender safe, the Hague Convention demands that when an army captures enemy soldiers, it should treat them well. Captured soldiers must give up their weapons, but they can keep their personal possessions. The army that captures them must feed and clothe them in the same manner that it would its own soldiers. When the war is over, the prisoners must be sent home as soon as possible.

The Red Cross

Jean Henri Dunant (1828–1910) was a Swiss lawyer who, while on a business trip, accidentally found himself at the **Battle** of Solferino in Italy. This battle, fought on June 24, 1859, was one of the bloodiest battles in European history. On that single day, 6,000 people were killed and 40,000 wounded. For three days and three nights, Dunant helped the local villagers care for wounded soldiers. He was horrified by the suffering caused by modern war, and sought to do something about it. In 1863 Dunant founded the Geneva Society for Public Welfare, which grew into the International Committee of the Red Cross (ICRC). The ICRC is an impartial, neutral, and independent organization whose mission is to protect the lives and dignity of victims of war and internal violence and to provide them with assistance. It also tries to prevent suffering by promoting and strengthening humanitarian law and universal humanitarian principles.

Preventing Conflicts

In 1945, following two world **wars,** nations no longer believed conflict was a legitimate way of achieving their aims. When the **United Nations** was created, its aim was to "spare future generations from the scourge of war." The UN charter basically said that only the United Nations could use force to solve conflict.

Although the aims of the United Nations were international peace and security, the first large-scale UN operation was a war. In 1950 North Korea invaded South Korea, and the United Nations joined the war on the side of South Korea. The **Soviet Union,** a member of the United Nations, and China, then not a member, joined the war on the side of North Korea. The Korean War was fought from 1950 to 1953, and although there was a **cease-fire** in 1953, the war has never formally been ended.

A peacekeeping force

In 1956 the UN conducted its first **peacekeeping** operation. Britain and France had convinced Israel to go to war against Egypt to keep the European hold on the Suez Canal. The British and the French wanted to "solve" the problem by sending their armies to separate the Egyptians and the Israelis. In the process Britain and France would take over the part of Egypt that controlled the important Suez Canal.

It soon became clear that the Israelis and Egyptians wanted to stop fighting, but each side needed to be sure that if they stopped, the other side would stop, too. What was needed was a neutral army to move between them, making it safe for both sides to stop fighting. The Egyptians, friends with the Soviet Union and China, would not accept a U.S. peacekeeping force. The Israelis, friends with the United States and Europe, would not accept Soviet peacekeepers. No one would accept the British and the French, because they had planned the war in the first place.

Eventually Lester Pearson, the Canadian foreign minister, suggested that a group of smaller countries could create a peacekeeping force under the UN banner. Both the Israelis and the Egyptians agreed. The first UN peacekeeping force consisted of soldiers from Canada, Sweden, and other countries. Because the

Canadian soldiers wore berets that made them look very much like British soldiers, the UN arranged for their berets to be replaced with helmets painted sky blue. Ever since, when soldiers go on UN duty, they take off their national hats or helmets and replace them with sky-blue UN headgear.

These people and vehicles were from different countries, but they were all part of the United Nations protection force in Sarajevo in 1995.

Other solutions

War is costly. The costs of war include people killed and injured, the resources spent on fighting, and resources destroyed by fighting. After wars are finished, humanitarian assistance and reconstruction can be expensive, too. Preventing conflict is easier and less expensive than fighting wars.

The difficulty is that people go to war when they see no alternative. It is often hard to find alternatives and compromises that both sides of a conflict will accept. This has made it difficult to prevent wars by bargaining and discussion. The **United Nations** and regional bodies such as the European Union, the Organization for African Unity, and the Organization of American States are dedicated to finding means to avoid war, but they are often unsuccessful.

Reducing the number of weapons

One means of preventing war is by agreeing to control **armament.** If states and groups keep their weapons stocks low enough, their neighbors will feel more secure and be less likely to consider war necessary. During the 1990s the tensions of the Cold War were calmed by the Conventional Forces in Europe Treaty, which carefully controlled the number and type of weapons that the former Cold War enemies could keep in Europe.

If countries are to buy fewer weapons, they need to be convinced that their enemies will not attack them. If they join together to guarantee each other's security by stationing multinational forces in danger zones and by being open with one another, different nations can come to feel more secure about their safety from attack.

Resolving conflicts

The best recent example of conflict resolution is South Africa. For many years up until the 1990s, South Africa's white population had used racist laws to discriminate against the majority black population. The whites feared that they would become victims if free elections were held and a black government was voted in. The whites were

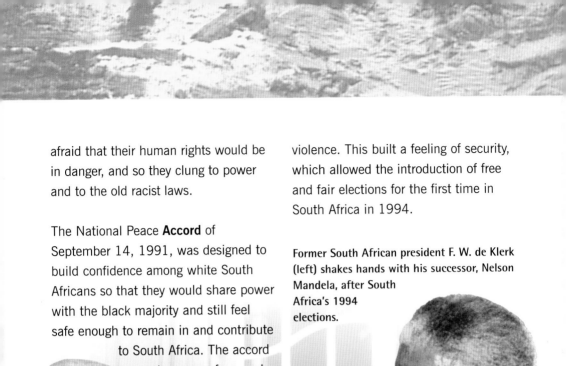

afraid that their human rights would be in danger, and so they clung to power and to the old racist laws.

The National Peace **Accord** of September 14, 1991, was designed to build confidence among white South Africans so that they would share power with the black majority and still feel safe enough to remain in and contribute to South Africa. The accord set up ways for people to solve their conflicts without violence. This built a feeling of security, which allowed the introduction of free and fair elections for the first time in South Africa in 1994.

Former South African president F. W. de Klerk (left) shakes hands with his successor, Nelson Mandela, after South Africa's 1994 elections.

War and Conflict and You

Some young people learn about the realities of **war** and conflict by participating in sea, air, or army cadet organizations. Cadets learn about leadership and adventure, but they also learn about soldiers and their way of life. This does not mean that they imagine war a pleasant or happy thing, just that the subject is something they want to learn about.

Organizations that seek to prevent war often encourage young people to participate in their programs. Many nations have **United Nations** associations, which sponsor such programs for young people. United Nations associations run Model United Nations events for young people, in which they learn about conflict resolution through role-playing and public speaking. Some even have summer camps where young people can come together to learn about the United Nations while also having fun. The United Nations Children's Fund, UNICEF, also has programs to involve young people in its work.

Many national Red Cross societies have youth organizations that teach young people about Red Cross work, both domestic and international. Red Cross societies welcome young

volunteers who can help relieve the suffering of war victims. For example, within only a few months of the beginning of the war in Afghanistan in 2001, U.S. children had raised $4 million for Afghan children in need.

People can use the Internet to learn more about conflict. The UN and other organizations have their own websites. Newspapers and broadcasters often provide links to those involved in the conflict on their sites. Regional organizations and **peacekeeping** forces usually have websites, and the people involved in the conflict often have websites of their own.

There are religious and political groups that campaign for conflict resolution and prevention. Other groups work to relieve war suffering, especially of children. These groups often change with issues and conflicts of the moment. Parents and teachers can help you to find appropriate groups to study or join.

Two girls collect donations for the American Red Cross in the aftermath of the World Trade Center bombing in 2001. Collecting for charity is just one way young people can be Red Cross volunteers.

Facts and Figures

Deaths in war—rough estimates

Number of **wars** fought in the 20th century 250

Number of people killed in war, 1901–2000 ....87.5 million

Number of wars fought, 1945–1995................................194

Number of people killed in war, 1945–1995 ....45 million

Number of wars, 1990–1995.........93

Number of people killed in war, 1990–1995 ....5.5 million

Money and war

Cost of fighting World War I...$186,333,637,000

World War I

Number of soldiers mobilized........................65,038,810

Number killed and died of wounds 8,538,315

Number wounded............21,219,452

Number missing and taken prisoner 7,750,919

Terrorism

Number of people killed in international **terrorist** attacks, 1990–1999 2,527

Number of people reported missing or dead after September 11, 2001 attacks in the United States. 2,823

Number of people killed by Palestinian terrorists in Israel in the fifteen years before the 1993 Israeli-Palestinian peace **accord** 254

Number of people killed by Palestinian terrorists in Israel in the five years after the 1993 Israeli-Palestinian peace accord 256

Land mines—rough estimates

Number of people killed or maimed in land mine explosions worldwide in 1999..................................26,000

Number of people killed or maimed in land mine explosions worldwide in 2000..................................20,000

Number of people killed or maimed in land mine explosions worldwide in 2001..................................10,000

Cost of buying one land mine....$3–$30

Cost of removing one land mine ....$300–$1,000

Further Information

Contacts

American Red Cross
431 18th Street NW
Washington, D.C. 20006
(202) 639-3520
www.redcross.org

Amnesty International
322 8th Avenue
New York, NY 10001
(212) 807-8400
e-mail: admin-us@aiusa.org
www.amnesty.org

CNN World News
One CNN Center
Atlanta, GA 30348
e-mail: cnn@cnn.com
www.cnn.com/world

UNICEF
UNICEF House
3 United Nations Plaza
New York, NY 10017
(212) 326-7000
e-mail: netmaster@unicef.org
www.unicef.org

United Nations
UN Headquarters
First Avenue at 46th Street
New York, NY 10017
www.un.org

United Nations Youth Unit
13th Floor, 2 UN Plaza
New York, NY 10017
(212) 963-2791
e-mail: ilenko@un.org
www.un.org/youth

Further reading

Anderson, Dale. *The Cold War Years.* Chicago: Raintree Publishers, 2001.

Cross, Robin. *Children and War: World War II.* Collingdale, Penn.: DIANE Publishing Company, 2002.

Giddens, Sandra. *Escape: Teens Who Escaped the Holocaust to Freedom.* New York: Rosen, 1999.

Kuhn, Betsy. *Angels of Mercy: The Army Nurses of World War II.* New York: Atheneum, 1999.

Nir, Yehuda. *The Lost Childhood: A World War II Memoir.* New York: Scholastic, 2002.

Opdyke, Irene Gut, and Jennifer Armstrong. *In My Hands: Memoirs of a Holocaust Survivor.* New York: Alfred A. Knopf, 1999.

Ross, Stewart. *Causes and Consequences of World War I.* Chicago: Raintree Publishers, 1998.

Ross, Stewart. *Causes of the Cold War.* Milwaukee: Gareth Stevens, 2002.

Saldinger, Anne Green. *Life In a Nazi Concentration Camp.* Farmington Hills, Mich.: Gale Group, 2000.

Torr, James D. *Americans' Views About War.* Farmington Hills, Mich.: Gale Group, 2001.

Glossary

accord   agreement or treaty between nations

allies   plural of **ally**

ally   person or state with whom you agree to join in defense against a common enemy

armament   tools used in defense from others or to attack others

atomic bomb   type of nuclear weapon that breaks the bonds that tie atoms together to release an immense amount of energy

Axis   alliance of Germany, Italy, and Japan during World War II

battle   fight between enemies who each mean to gain a strategic advantage. Other kinds of fights include raids and sieges.

biological warfare   warfare that uses germs (bacteria or viruses) to make the enemy ill or to kill the enemy

capitalism   economic system based on private ownership (by business, industry, etc.) rather than on public or government ownership

Cathar   member of a religious group in southern Europe in the late 1100s and early 1200s

cavalry   soldiers who fight primarily on horseback

cease-fire   agreement by both sides in a conflict to stop fighting, usually temporary

chemical weapon   weapon that uses poison to make the enemy ill or to kill the enemy

civilian   person not in the armed forces

Commonwealth of Nations   voluntary association of independent nations, most of which used to be ruled by Britain

communism   economic system based on public (government) ownership, rather than that of business (private) ownership

convention   treaty agreed on by several nations

conventional   weapons or methods of war customarily used throughout history until recently

cult   religious group set up to gain money or power for its leader(s)

dictator   ruler who is not restricted by laws and will not tolerate official opposition

ethnic group   group of people who share a common culture, a common language, or believe they share a common ancestry

genocide   deliberate killing of a nation of people or an ethnic group

guerrilla   person who fights in secret against a more powerful enemy

heresy   idea that goes against accepted religious teaching

hoplite   Classical Greek armored foot soldier

hydrogen bomb   type of nuclear weapon in which atoms of hydrogen are fused together to produce helium, releasing tremendous energy. Hydrogen bombs are more powerful than atomic bombs.

Industrial Revolution   change during the 1700s and 1800s from an agricultural to an industrial economy

irregulars   soldiers who follow looser rules than **regulars**

just cause policy or idea that is considered morally right

just war war believed morally correct to fight

League of Nations organization formed in 1920 to encourage nations to settle their differences peacefully

massacre killing of many people

merchant ship ship intended to carry passengers and cargo

militia people who are organized to fight, but are not part of regular armies (*see* regular army)

NATO North Atlantic Treaty Organization, formed in 1949 as an alliance of Western European nations plus Iceland, the United States, and Canada. The NATO countries promise to defend each other against threats from other nations.

Nazi Germany Germany when it was controlled by the National Socialist German Workers' Party (between 1934 and 1945)

peacekeeper soldier sent to keep soldiers from other countries from fighting, usually as part of a United Nations peacekeeping mission

Palestine Liberation Organization (PLO) formed in 1964 from a union of several Arab groups with the aim of creating a state for Palestinian Arabs and removing the State of Israel

refugee person seeking refuge from war or persecution

regular armies of soldiers who are expected to follow rules. Regular soldiers are generally paid, and fight for their own countries.

reservist civilian who is trained to join a regular army in times of emergency

shell munition designed to be fired from an artillery piece, or very large gun

Soviet Union Union of Soviet Socialist Republics, or Soviet Union, formed in 1922 from the former Russian Empire. The Soviet Union was dissolved in 1991.

systematic according to a plan

telegraph means of communication by electrical impulses sent over wires

terrorism deliberate and systematic murder, maiming, and menacing of the innocent to inspire fear for political ends

terrorist person who used terrorism

theologian person who studies the nature and practice of religious faith

transfer of population also called "ethnic cleansing." Forcibly moving a group of people from one area to another for political reasons

treaty agreement between nations

tribunal court, usually military

truce cease-fire

United Nations (UN) voluntary association of countries that join together to promote international peace and security

war conflict intended to achieve political aims by using armed forces to attack and destroy an enemy's resources or armed forces

war crime violation of the laws of war, or a crime against humanity (such as genocide) committed during war

Index